BRITAIN'S ♜ HERITAGE

The 1950s Home

Janet Shepherd and John Shepherd

AMBERLEY

Acknowledgements

Every attempt has been made to seek permission for copyright material used in this book. However, if we have inadvertently used copyright material without permission/ acknowledgement we apologise and we will make the necessary correction at the first opportunity.

The authors would like to thank the following for their kind assistance in the completion of this book: Lisa-Marie Beddis at Getty Archives, Pat Carter, Brenda Corn, Mark Dunton and Paul Johnson at the National Archives, Tim Hayward, Sally Jones, Simon Jones, Sandra Lee, Karen Livingstone, Vivien Mathieson, Pete Mulvey, Christine Parry, Ken Parry, Celia Tyler at the Cambridgeshire Collection, Dr Christopher Walker.

Finally, a very special word of thanks to Les Waters and Rose Waters for expert technical assistance, advice and patience; and to our commissioning editor, Nick Wright, for invaluable help and support. Any remaining errors and omissions are entirely the authors' responsibility.

About the Authors

Dr Janet Shepherd gained her doctorate in Poor Law education at London Guildhall University. She is co-author with John Shepherd of *1920s Britain* (2010), *1970s Britain* (2012) and *1950s Childhood* (2014) for Shire Books, and is currently working on a history of a little known radical twentieth century society, the Progressive League.

Professor John Shepherd has worked at the University of Huddersfield since 2010, and was previously joint director of the Labour History Research Unit at Anglia Ruskin University in Cambridge. His publications include *Crisis? What Crisis: the Callaghan Government and the British Winter of Discontent* (MUP, 2013).

First published 2017

Amberley Publishing
The Hill, Stroud
Gloucestershire, GL5 4EP

www.amberley-books.com

Copyright © Janet Shepherd and
John Shepherd, 2017

The right of Janet Shepherd and John Shepherd to be identified as the Authors of this work has been asserted in accordance with the Copyrights, Designs and Patents Act 1988.

ISBN 978 1 4456 6568 9 (paperback)
ISBN 978 1 4456 6569 6 (ebook)

British Library Cataloguing in Publication Data.
A catalogue record for this book is available from the British Library.

Printed in the UK.

Contents

1

Introduction: From Austerity to Affluence

During the post-Second World War years, the provision of housing, both public and private, was a major issue in British politics and national recovery. The 1950s was a highly significant decade when the years of austerity gradually turned into affluence based on full employment, welfare state services and the relative prosperity of a consumer society imbued with rising expectations. The fortunate generation born after the Second World War, mainly in the 1950s, now known as the 'baby boomers', are currently reaching retirement age in the second decade of the twenty-first century. This book explores the homes into which they were raised during some of the most interesting years of change in post-war Britain.

The national housing stock was already inadequate and often lacked modern amenities. During the Second World War, 4 million homes had been destroyed by enemy bombing, particularly in the major cities, industrial centres and ports, including London, Liverpool, Glasgow, Birmingham, Manchester, Newcastle, Southampton, Portsmouth and Bristol. House building ceased during the war, adding to a shortage of around 1.25 million homes, chiefly in the public sector. The post-war increase in the birth rate compounded an already difficult state of affairs. National and local government was faced with major problems: slum clearance, the provision of an adequate supply of new homes and renovated properties, as well the demand for new schools and hospitals for an increasing population.

For many people, the cessation of hostilities initially brought few changes. Wartime identity cards were not rescinded until 1952 and, before rationing finally ceased in 1954, there were continuing restrictions, notably on food but also on furniture, textiles and crockery. Clothing was de-rationed in 1949 but choice remained limited. The bulk of the population had little disposable income. For some, conditions were even worse after the war. From 1946, certain impoverished British families received food aid from the USA and Canada.

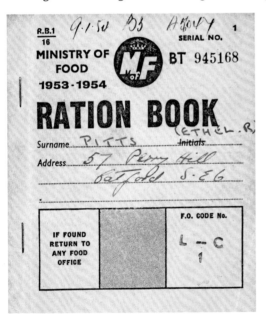

In the early 1950s, most food was still rationed. Meat was the final item to come off ration in 1954. (Janet Shepherd)

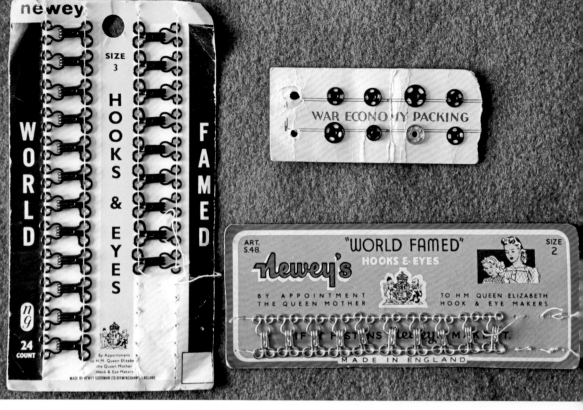

Above: The wartime adage 'Make Do and Mend' continued into the early 1950s. Newey's Hooks & Eyes were 'by appointment to H. M. The Queen Mother'. (Janet Shepherd)

Right: Wood and paper continued to be in short supply in the early years. A 1950 dolls' house was made out of an old orange box. (Janet Shepherd)

Did you know?

A typical adult weekly grocery ration in 1950: 50 grams each of butter, cheese, jam, tea; 100 grams of margarine, bacon/ham; 225 grams sugar and one fresh egg. One packet of dried egg and 350 grams of sweets were allowed monthly. Sweets were first de-rationed in 1949 but stocks were so quickly exhausted that rationing was re-introduced and not finally removed until February 1953.

Inadequate housing compounded the problems faced by many households. In the inner cities, bomb sites and slums dominated the landscape. Although middle-class suburban homes built by private contractors had mushroomed in the inter-war years, many Britons still occupied homes built in the late nineteenth and early twentieth centuries. Nearly half the population were in poor, privately rented accommodation. In London, a fifth of the housing stock was classified as slum. Numerous street parties for the coronation of Queen Elizabeth II in 1953 were held in bombed-out areas. Millions of poor homes lacked the basic amenities of heating and plumbing. Toilets were mostly outside and shared. Coal and coke fires continually belched dust and fumes into the atmosphere, resulting in pollution that led to dense fogs, memorably the 1952 'London Smog'.

In the 1950s, public authorities dominated both the theory and practice of reconstruction, providing unique opportunities for architects, town planners and designers. Between 1945 and 1951, the Labour government recognised the urgent need for high quality housing as an integral part of its new, comprehensive welfare state. Aneurin Bevan, Minister for Health and Housing, promoted an idealistic vision for new council estates where 'the working man, the doctor and the clergyman will live in close proximity to each other'. A huge building programme was instituted, which later peaked under the Conservatives. Re-development schemes in major cities and towns brought a different mid-twentieth-century vision of house building and home life.

Dear Sir,

In reply to your letter I wish to state that most I could offer is £1200.

The house itself is in a deplorable state it wants a new roof and also new guttering. The inside of the house wants painting and new paper. The gas stove has nearly had it and there is not a decent fire-place in the house. The washhouse under the house wants a new copper and the wooden tubs have a big hole in them and have to be stuffed up with rag to make them hold water. To get the house up to anywhere near decent it would cost in the vicinity of £1000. for improvements.

In regards of signing an agreement to increase rental with all these repairs needed doing I cannot see my way clear to agree.

1952 complaint about the state of a rental property that needed substantial work – a new roof, guttering, 'decent' fireplaces and redecoration. (Janet Shepherd)

Multiple occupancy terraced housing in Gothic Street, Cambridge, 1950s. Few cars and gardens meant children played in the street. (Cambridgeshire Collection)

Middle-class housing. Hilda Parry and her daughter Hilary outside their substantial inter-war semi-detached house, in Meadow Lane, Worsley, Lancashire, c. 1952. (Ken Parry)

Above: 1950s coal shute. Coal was poured down the shute directly into the bunker in the family kitchen. Woodberry Down Estate, Stoke Newington. Photograph, 2016. (John Shepherd) **Left**: A regular 1950s household bill. Many 1950s children recall their parents instructing them to count the bags of coal and coke as the coalman emptied the sacks into home bunkers. (Janet Shepherd)

The decade saw a combination of extensive council building, with low- and high-rise blocks, prefabricated factory-built single-storey buildings, known as 'prefabs', and some private homes. Over the decade, of the 2.45 million homes that were constructed, two-thirds were local authority housing, including large-scale new estates. Woodberry Down in Stoke Newington was the biggest London County Council (LCC) estate, constructed in the post-war years mainly to re-house slum dwellers from neighbouring boroughs. The desire for a new start was boosted by the 1951 Festival of Britain where bold, contemporary designs were evident in textiles, furniture, crockery and, most notably, in its 'living architecture' project, the Lansbury housing estate in London's East End.

From the early 1950s, the dominant architectural choice became 'New Brutalism' or 'New Modernism', known also as 'brutalist' or 'modernist' architecture and characterised by the use of heavy concrete slabs. Pioneered by the Swiss-French architect Le Corbusier, this approach was famously used by Sir Basil Spence in the new Coventry Cathedral, built between 1951 and 1962, which later became an iconic international symbol of post-war reconstruction. Modernist styles were frequently chosen for public buildings, notably the Royal Festival Hall, and also for council, and some private, housing. Urban expansion in the inter-war years had been unregulated and the 1946 New Towns Act, and 1947 Town and Country Planning Act, offered centrally planned solutions to inner-city housing problems. Re-development schemes became especially radical in major cities, while the creation of new towns, such as Hemel Hempstead and Peterlee, brought a different approach.

By the mid-to-late 1950s, with full employment bringing greater prosperity, a modern consumer society developed. Wartime 'utility' schemes for clothes, crockery and furniture

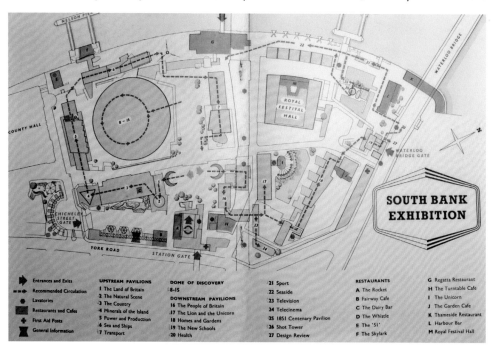

South Bank layout, Festival of Britain, 1951. The rectangular Homes and Gardens pavilion was on the edge of the site, below Waterloo Bridge gate.

Above: The Post Office's colourful stamps commemorated 100 years between the Great Exhibition, 1851, and the 1951 Festival of Britain. (Reproduced by kind permission of The Royal Mail Group Ltd)
Left: A Festival of Britain metal commemorative souvenir teapot, with a bakelite handle and decorated with stars, a lion and a crown. (Janet Shepherd)

ended in 1952. New materials like plastic and nylon revolutionised home interiors, as labour-saving gadgets and bright fabrics became affordable. The latest medium of television expanded rapidly after 1953, when millions of people crowded into their own, or other people's, homes to watch the Coronation and also the memorable 'Stanley Matthews' 1953 FA Cup Final. By the close of the decade, the growth in car ownership meant that householders increasingly sought homes with garages. More leisure time led to a passion for 'Do It Yourself' (DIY) and a growing desire for gardens.

The authors, Janet and John Shepherd, were both brought up during the 1950s, an important decade rich in continuities and contrasts in home life. This volume, which draws on a wide range of oral, documentary and media sources, explores a fascinating range of key aspects of the 1950s home at a time of significant developments in British society.

Christine Watson sitting astride the family motorbike in 1953. Cut-out crowns were fixed onto the garden shed to celebrate the Coronation. (Christine Parry)

Janet's 1950s home, with twenty-six rooms, Wimborne Road, Bournemouth. Built in 1865, demolished and replaced by flats in 2000. Photograph, 1999. (Janet Shepherd)

One of the major blocks on the LCC's Woodberry Down Estate. The estate was built during the 1950s and still occupied in 2016. (John Shepherd)

2

Planning for the Future

Housing reconstruction was a major social and political issue in the 1950s. The uncontrolled inter-war expansion of suburbia, followed by the wartime cessation of house building, meant strategic planning was seen as essential. This was considerably enabled by the 1947 Town and Country Planning Act, which introduced a centralised system whereby newly formed and re-organised local authorities were able to control and plan all future building in their areas.

By 1955, nearly half the country's architects were employed designing public buildings and council houses. Opinions diverged between those who saw Britain's future in subsidised city re-development, often replacing slums with high-rise blocks, and those who wanted to build outside cities, in green suburbs and new towns.

Did you know?

American singer Rosemary Clooney recorded two hit songs about houses, 'Come On-a My House' (1950) and 'This Ole House' (1954), which reached the top of both UK and USA pop charts: 'This ole house is a-gettin' shaky, this ole house is a-gettin' old ... ain't got time to oil the hinges nor to mend the window pane ...'

1950s housing plans were enriched by ideas emanating from the 1951 Festival of Britain, with its emphasis on 'good design'. This was the first national post-war event, promising a bright, colourful future after the drab, grey war years. When the Festival opened on London's South Bank, with its twenty-five pavilions and monolithic Royal Festival Hall, wartime utility restrictions were coming to an end. Dull clothing, utilitarian furniture and plain white china were being replaced by vivid colours and modern styles.

In the Homes Pavilion, houses of the future were displayed with folding walls, movable screens, open side-boards, shelving units, dining recesses and practical serving hatches. However, it was the Festival's innovative design for the newly created Lansbury estate that would become a better forecast of future trends in housing than the more 'exuberant South Bank architecture'.

After the war, planners and builders were hampered by the paucity of materials. Wartime restrictions on timber importation continued well into the 1950s and steel supplies remained limited. This was compounded by a labour shortage. Architects were forced to maximise space and consider carefully how each home would function. The major influence came from Le Corbusier, Swiss pioneer of the school of Modern architecture. Le Corbusier was renowned before the war but his greatest influence in Britain came in the 1950s. He received the Royal Institute of Architects' prestigious Gold Medal for outstanding architectural achievements in 1953. His approach advocated concrete blocks

Right: The 1951 Festival of Britain's Southbank with brightly coloured building and umbrellas. Festival Hall is at the back of the lower image. **Below**: The 1950 plan for Poplar, later to be the Lansbury Estate, with housing, churches, schools (Catholic and Protestant), an old people's home and community centre. (The National Archives)

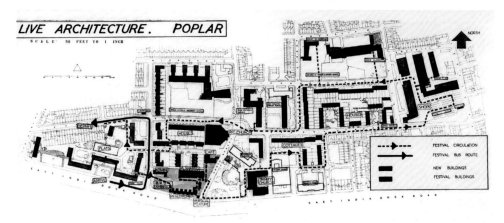

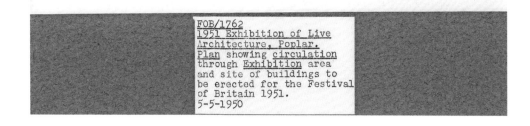

FOB/1762
1951 Exhibition of Live
Architecture, Poplar.
Plan showing circulation
through Exhibition area
and site of buildings to
be erected for the Festival
of Britain 1951.
5-5-1950

of high-rise flats, seen as an effective means to achieve density housing through the economical mass production of building materials. Concrete was the favoured product, becoming synonymous with 'modernistic' architecture.

Did you know?

Enemy bombing had destroyed Coventry Cathedral in 1940. In 1950, Basil Spence's winning modernistic design for a new cathedral controversially linked it with the ruins of the old building. It later received world-wide commendation and was Grade I listed in 1998.

Le Corbusier's theories and emphasis on communal living were incorporated in much 1950s architecture. Rather than concentrate on individual wants, he believed multiple occupants would co-operate to improve their mutual environment. Notable converts to his 'slab block' style were architects Alison and Peter Smithson. The Smithsons coined the evocative phrase 'streets in the sky' to describe high blocks of flats but this term later became associated with evolving problems on high-rise estates. Other Le Corbusier aficionados included: Frederick Gibberd, notable designer of the Lansbury Estate and, later, The Lawn, Britain's first residential high-rise in Harlow New Town; also Powell and Moya, who included a preponderance of reinforced concrete in their ultra-modern plans to replace war-damaged Victorian housing in Pimlico's Churchill Gardens estate. Their design included alternate high

Birmingham City Surveyor and Engineer, Herbert Manzoni, and City Architect A. G. Sheppard Fidler, with the model of Birmingham's Inner Ring Road scheme, 1954. It comprised a modernistic outer ring of high-rise blocks, later nicknamed a 'concrete collar'. (Getty Images)

and low blocks, maisonettes, terraced houses and children's play areas. Sited on a north/south axis to maximise sunlight, Churchill Gardens remains a unique modernistic example, becoming Grade II listed in 1998.

Architect R. A. Livett's modern design for Leeds' Saxton Gardens estate incorporated 448 flats in blocks of five to ten storeys. Initially a vociferous proponent of high-rise living, Livett later changed his opinion. Birmingham's City Surveyor and Engineer, Herbert Manzoni, however, remained a lifelong convert. His drastic slum clearance plan, following Birmingham's wartime devastation, would replace insanitary back-to-back housing with high-rise blocks.

The country's need for new, subsidised, public housing was soon evident to the incoming 1945 government. The Housing brief fell to the Health Minister, idealistic Aneurin Bevan. Bevan had already spearheaded the establishment of Britain's Health Service (NHS) and was a lifelong campaigner for social justice. His housing goal was quality council accommodation: 'nothing ... was considered too good for the workers'. He had already collaborated with town planner Thomas Sharp on a 1949 inner city *Housing Manual*. Bevan wanted council accommodation that compared favourably with the private sector, homes 'he and his fellow ministers would be happy to live in'. Originally, it was thought 750,000 homes would suffice, comprising newly built flats, houses on estates, repaired or converted existing homes and new towns. However, this proved a vast underestimate as eventually several million were needed. The urgent housing problem meant Bevan reluctantly had to accept the speedier, economical plan of temporary prefabricated housing, first adopted during the war. Relatively cheap and easy to construct, 'prefabs', made in factories but assembled on site, would prove a practical solution to ease the post-war housing shortage. Unexpectedly, they became both long-lasting and popular.

With resources in short supply, Bevan imposed stringent controls on the private sector. Opportunities for private building in the early 1950s were limited by building regulations that channelled scarce materials and resources into council housing and schools as social

Britain's first purpose-built community clinic under construction on Woodberry Down Estate. It had a range of facilities including eye, dental and child guidance clinics plus a minor operations room. (John Shepherd)

need was prioritised over market forces. Once compensation had been paid to owners, local authorities could compulsorily acquire bombsites for re-development. Almost 90 per cent of British homes built from 1945 to 1951 were local authority builds. It was further recognised that communal facilities were essential to support the extensive new housing.

Labour's plans to build for posterity emphasised quality over quantity. Building made slow progress as the *right* type of housing was prioritised over *any* housing. The general public, however, just wanted houses to live in. Labour eventually built about a million homes, some subsequently called 'Bevan estates', averaging 200,000 a year. The incoming 1951 Conservative government determined to exceed Labour's record. The new Housing Minister, Harold Macmillan, criticised Labour's slow progress, complaining that, for example, in the new town of Basildon there was 'no water, no sewerage and jolly few houses'. Macmillan's

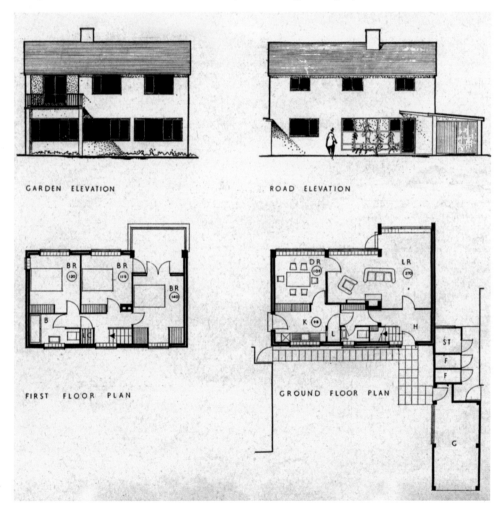

Harlow Design Group's plans for detached houses at The Glebelands, Harlow, in *The Architect and Building News*, July 1952.

goal was to erect an annual 300,000 'houses for the people'. Subsidies for local authorities were increased, encouraging more publically funded projects.

Through changes in building and planning controls, Macmillan also actively encouraged private enterprise. Private builders and developers were arguably better at assessing the needs of the housing market, only producing the number of homes they could realistically sell. Under 1950s administrations, private housing grew steadily. One of the most progressive private firms was Span, who specialised in providing attractive middle-income homes. The name was chosen to 'span the gap' between repetitive suburbia and individually designed architects' houses.

While some planners and architects supported inner-city re-development, others favoured new towns. The most notable advocate was town planner Patrick Abercrombie. His ambitious 1944 *Greater London Plan*, together with Thomas Sharp's *Town Planning* (1946), became a blueprint for future new town developments. Published in a blaze of publicity, Abercrombie proposed dividing the capital into four rings: inner urban, suburban, a protected green belt and finally, an outer ring. A million people would be dispersed from the inner area to new satellite towns in the outer ring. Abercrombie's vision became the catalyst for new towns in the 1950s, highlighting the need not only for better housing, but also for improved sanitation, open spaces and infrastructure. Plans for eleven new English towns and three in Scotland

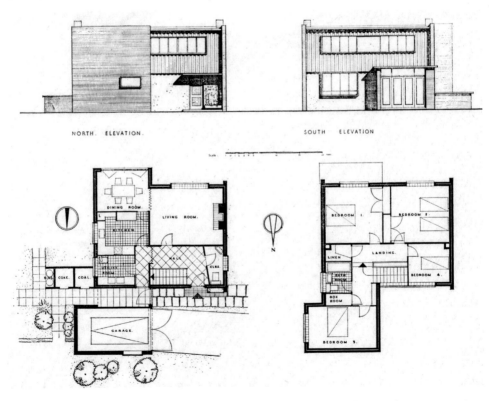

NORTH. ELEVATION.   SOUTH ELEVATION

Design for an 'upper-income-group' Wimpey house, Harlow. Four bedrooms, boxroom, spacious downstairs living areas, coke and coal bunkers and a garage. *Architect and Building News*, July 1952.

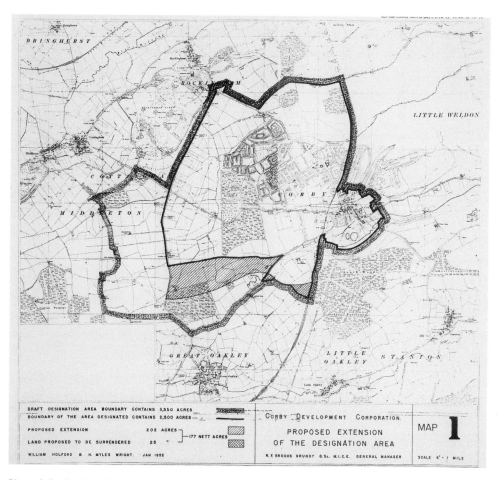

Plan of Corby New Town in 1952. The lined section shows a proposed extension, encompassing a further 202 acres. (The National Archives)

were accepted between 1946 and 1955. Of these, eight were designed to circle the capital to accommodate London's population overspill.

During the 1950s, as plans for new towns evolved alongside designs for inner-city high-rise blocks, each had its passionate supporters and detractors. Town planner Frederic Osborn disliked 'vertical living' and was astonished that England, 'the envied country of the family home with garden', should favour 'increasingly piling houses on top of each other'. Harold Macmillan, however, publically advocated building upwards and the *Daily Mirror* agreed, stating, 'The country must live in flats'. The high-rise concept attracted many young architects looking for a challenge. Later R. A. Livett acknowledged that most people preferred semi-detached rather than high-rise living but his change of heart came too late to prevent high flats going up in Leeds. In due course, mainly in the 1960s, tower blocks would prove unpopular and in some instances unsafe, but in the 1950s the views of tenants were low down planners' lists of priorities.

Above: Architects Fry, Drew & Partners' early 1950s plans for flats in Tony's Dell, Harlow, included balconies and, unusually, central heating.
Right: This Oxo advertisement appeared in 1950, when the security of 'home and hearth' was very important after wartime uncertainty. (Premier Foods)

IT'S AN ODD HOUSE

WHERE THERE'S NO

3
Post-War Reconstruction

Post-war reconstruction presented a daunting task for both planners and the building industry in the 1950s. Major cities were in desperate need of rebuilding, especially in London after the devastation caused by the Blitz. Slum clearance was a major and ambitious undertaking. A considerable amount of existing inner-city housing had been neglected and was in a state of poor repair, unsuited to the post-war world. Only a third of homes were owner occupied. The majority of working-class households rented rooms, bedsits or flats in houses that were owned, and often neglected, by landlords who themselves lived elsewhere.

As part of central government's wholesale planning, landlords could apply for improvement grants to modernise rental properties, resulting in some renovations and conversions, often into yet more flats and bedsits. Not all areas had suffered bombing but living conditions remained poor. By 1951, only 21 per cent of homes in Stepney, East London, had piped water, cooking stoves, kitchen sinks, fixed baths and adequate heating. Housing in many cities was mostly comprised of older properties, much of it from the previous century.

Demolishing old terraced housing in Emmanuel Street, Cambridge, while a shop remains open at the other end. Early 1950s. (Cambridgeshire Collection)

Above left: Janet's grandmother rented two rooms here, above the bay window, in 1950. The shared toilet was on the second floor. Aberdeen Road, Highbury. Photograph, 2007. (Janet Shepherd)
Above right: The view down Aberdeen Road in 2007 remained virtually unchanged apart from the parked cars. Most houses had multiple occupancy in 1950. (Janet Shepherd)

Did you know?

Singer Cilla Black recalled that her mother desperately wanted to move from the family's rented flat above a Liverpool barber's shop. The flat was later modernised, including a new bathroom, but all Cilla's mother wanted was a 'two up two down terrace', with her own front door.

It was not only city living that was poor and inadequate. Rural areas also suffered from poverty as wages were particularly low. Most farmers still employed lowly paid agricultural labourers who lived in tied cottages. This meant that, if their jobs came to an end, they also lost their homes. Rural accommodation frequently lacked modern sanitation and was often the last to be linked to the electricity grid.

In the urgent need for reconstruction, architects' visions were not always evident in practice. Some 1950s properties began to be characterised by a concrete, urban sludge-grey look, a far cry from the Festival of Britain's vision of a colourful future. Limited land availability, building materials and labour meant new post-war homes were inevitably smaller.

Many houses were quick to assemble, requiring less skilled labour than traditional methods, and there were criticisms of poor workmanship and doing things 'on the cheap'. Both council and private builders used prefabricated concrete. Well-known firms like Wates,

Left: Many rural homes were often very isolated. Few households had cars, and residents had to depend on infrequent buses. (Janet Shepherd)

Below: The concrete, modernistic, Royal Festival Hall was the Festival's only permament, and later world famous, building. Grade I listed, 1981.

Laing and Wimpey all used large amounts of 'pre-cast reinforced concrete', commonly called PRC, not always due to choice but also because brick production was only just returning to pre-war levels. As production levels gradually increased, brick began to be used again, alongside concrete. Two-storey, red-brick terraced houses began to appear in many towns across Britain.

Above: Wisbey builders from nearby Haslingfield, constructing a large estate of brick council houses in Medcalf Way, Melbourn, Cambridgeshire, 1950s. (Cambridgeshire Collection)
Right: 1950s houses in Medcalf Way, Melbourn, still occupied in 2016. Some have remained as council rentals, others are privately owned. (Karen Livingstone)

Simpler designs replaced elaborate pre-war styles. Bay and leaded windows, for example, were discarded in favour of wider, plainer steel frames. Roofs were shallower, front porches simpler. Homes generally had two or three bedrooms, a merged dining/living room, internal toilet and a fitted kitchen with stainless steel sinks. Concrete floors were often covered in linoleum, especially in kitchens. The traditional pre-war front 'parlour' gradually disappeared. Costs were reduced as less wood was needed. Before the dangers were realised, asbestos was commonly used for thermal insulation in roofs throughout the 1950s and also for gutters, piping, garages and sheds.

Above: 1950s neighbours chat over the fence. Mid-terrace and end-of-terrace council homes, with commonly styled front porches. (Sandra Lee)
Left: Both front and internal doors had fewer panels and embellishments after the war, when timber was still in short supply. (Janet Shepherd)

Oak Crescent. A group of well-maintained semi-detached 1950s council houses and gardens, still cared for and occupied in 2016. (Janet Shepherd)

Many new council homes were prefabs, mostly detached, composed of concrete, steel and aluminium. In Stevenage, prefabs were used not just for housing but also as temporary work buildings for the many people employed in establishing the new town. The Ministry of Works produced several prefab designs, none more than 7 feet, 5 inches wide (2.261 metres) as they had to be transported by road. They were surprisingly spacious, often with better facilities than traditional houses. Each possessed mains electricity, hot and cold running water, an entrance hall, two bedrooms with built-in wardrobes, a heated bathroom, toilet, a fitted kitchen with a built-in refrigerator, a living room and a small garden. Kitchens and bathrooms were arranged back-to-back for ease of plumbing. Prefabs were designed to last ten years but many remained well beyond that time, some even surviving into the next century. Complaints about thin walls and continual condensation were generally superseded by the joys of indoor plumbing and private garden plots. The description 'Palaces for the People' took hold and prefabs became widespread across all parts of the country. In the popular television series *Foyle's War*, post-war episodes featured Samantha and MP husband Andrew beginning their married life in a prefab.

Council estates first began to appear in the inter-war years. The world's largest, most ambitious public housing estate first began at Becontree in the London Borough of Barking and Dagenham in the 1920s. Known as a country estate, Becontree differed by being mainly composed of houses and gardens rather than blocks of flats. During the 1950s, the expansion of Ford UK's mammoth Dagenham car plant led to a further 600 homes being added from 1949 to 1951, as observed in the 2010 film *Made in Dagenham*.

Did you know?

English contemporary artist, George Shaw's paintings of Tile Hill, an open-plan 'Bevan estate' in Coventry, were nominated for the prestigious Turner prize in 2011. Unusually, Shaw worked with model paint commonly used for model kits like Airfix.

1950s prefabs, Excalibur Estate in Catford, London, still occupied in 2015. Great care was taken to maintain the small gardens. (Getty Images)

The estates that arose in the 1950s differed from the majority of those built before the war by providing modern facilities, most notably indoor sanitation. However, progress was often slow. Some parts of Liverpool were re-developed fairly quickly, but Lorna Sage (*Bad Blood*, 2000) recalled bombed tenements still waiting for demolition and re-development in 1953. Several Newcastle estates were particularly slow to receive modern amenities.

One of the most innovative estates was the Lansbury in Poplar and Stepney, part of London's deprived East End. This was the LCC's showcase estate, a lasting practical legacy from the Festival of Britain, created on a heavily bombed thirty acre site and named after inter-war Labour leader George Lansbury. A 'modern oasis set in a vast area of overcrowded streets', commented *The Sphere* in June 1951. It included 'neighbourhood units' comprising maisonettes and terraced houses, low blocks for elderly residents, schools, churches and a pedestrianised shopping centre. London brick was utilised in addition to concrete, giving a softer look, and the non-regimented, irregular layout was later adopted in other city centres, estates and new towns.

The LCC's Woodberry Down estate in Stoke Newington, North London, established 1946–1962, was generally more typical of post-war local authority large-scale social housing. The estate's residents were mainly moved from slums in Shoreditch, Hackney, Islington and similar poor neighbourhoods in the bombed metropolis. Families were re-housed in basic living accommodation, ranging from one bedroom to four bedroom flats that often proved too cramped for modern living. However, the first reaction was generally favourable, particularly with the provision of a bathroom and a separate indoor toilet, as well as a communal room in each block for drying washing. There were also pram sheds in the courtyard for storage.

Planning for Woodberry Down had begun in the mid-1930s, when the Labour LCC envisaged a major working-class 'estate of the future' on a compulsorily purchased sixty-four acre site near an affluent middle-class part of Stoke Newington. It received hostile opposition from the municipal council, local businesses and nearby wealthier residents and the Second World War delayed construction. Architects planning Woodberry Down had toured contemporary European public housing schemes. Their eventual choice was a group of five-storey blocks,

Another block on the large Woodberry Down council estate. The Shepherd family of six lived in a first floor flat. Photograph, 2016. (John Shepherd)

with lifts and long balconies providing walking access. Six other taller, eight-storey, concrete buildings included more expensive flats with central heating. Altogether there was provision for 2,500 families.

The estate had several assets, including a local authority direct labour force of builders and decorators, as well as local resident caretakers, gardeners and rent collectors, responsible for maintenance. A parade of shops, a primary school, a new branch library, a public house and, most notably, the Health Centre opened in 1952. From 1955, Woodberry Down Secondary School, one of the earliest purpose-built post-war comprehensives under its renowned first Head, Harriet Chetwynd, attracted students both from the estate and further afield. Parts of the estate had a pleasant, open aspect, bordering the New River and two nearby Victorian reservoirs that provided drinking water for the capital. However, the reservoirs were prohibited to the estate's tenants in the 1950s and were regularly patrolled by security guards with dogs.

Woodberry Down was a brave utopian venture to develop a new housing estate, with a community heart, for working families. However, some poor designs detracted from daily life. Younger children were only provided with a couple of small play areas and older children rarely found anywhere quiet to study, often tackling homework on the living room floor. By the close of the decade, the courtyards between the blocks became increasingly overcrowded as car ownership took hold. Similarly, later 1950s consumerism, with refrigerators, washing machines and other household appliances, had not been envisaged. Water penetration was a frequent and recurring problem. After the on-site labour force was withdrawn in the 1980s, the material fabric of the estate soon declined. Over sixty years since its construction, Woodberry Down remains a council estate, albeit with a mixture of public and private accommodation. In 2016, a controversial private and local authority gentrification scheme evolved to attract new residents. The new creation of Woodberry Down wetlands dramatically changed the environment. Residents can now walk by the New River, view its bird sanctuary and aquatic life, and sail on the West Reservoir.

As the 1950s progressed, the regeneration trend was resolutely upwards. In 1952, West Ham retracted its four-storey limitation and agreed to a ten-tier block. A similar approach was adopted in Manchester and Liverpool; only a few councils like Salford retained a seven-storey limit. All council-built flats received similar housing grants until 1956, when new funding was disproportionately weighted in favour of blocks over six storeys high. This encouraged authorities to build even higher and, in London, council house construction re-doubled. Three times as much subsidy was then allowed for a flat than for a house. In Sheffield, with scant regard for the needs of tenants, a huge post-war programme to re-house slum families on the Park Hill council estate (1957–61) included blocks of fifteen or more tiers.

Not all new housing blocks were inadequate. Whereas the worst resembled Victorian tenements, the best, particularly those built by more progressive councils, were spacious and well-equipped, with fitted bathrooms and immersion heaters. A few possessed central heating, although most still used coke and coal. Kitchens had built-in larders and sometimes a choice between gas and electric cookers. The most desired amenities were serving hatches and individual balconies. Communal basement areas were common but garages rare as few residents possessed cars until the close of the decade.

The massive task of post-war reconstruction meant social housing became inevitably numbers driven and the human element was often disregarded. Many families re-housed to the top of high-rise blocks experienced soul-destroying isolation and depression, while poor insulation could mean intrusive noise from neighbours. The sometime crippling effects from high-rise living were not, however, fully recognised during the 1950s.

In some instances, it was considered easier to create new towns on open land rather than clear inner city slums and rebuild. Several new towns were built after the war to absorb some of London's growing population. Stevenage in 1946 was followed by Harlow, Crawley and Hemel Hempstead a year later. Stevenage established neighbourhood units, similar to the Lansbury estate, for 5–10,000 people. Hemel Hempstead became a garden city on the lines of Welwyn Garden City, founded in the 1920s. New English towns outside the capital were Aycliffe and Peterlee in County Durham (1947/8), Bracknell in Berkshire (1949) and

Brandon Estate, Southwark, 1959. 'London's tallest flats, almost ready for occupation.' Prospective tenants lived in temporary prefabs awaiting completion. (Getty Images)

Corby, Northamptonshire, in 1950. Peterlee was unique in being built following a request by local residents, mainly miners, for a new town. In Scotland, Glenrothes (1948) was created to house miners from the new Rothes Colliery, while East Kilbride (1947) and Cumbernauld (1955) provided much needed housing for Glasgow's overspill. Although the new town of Milton Keynes did not appear until the 1960s, neighbouring Bletchley expanded rapidly in the post-war years as families migrated from North London, where the housing situation was poor and jobs more scarce.

The new towns that appeared after the war contained both low- and high-rise housing. Apart from notable exceptions such as Harlow's Lawn block, only ten per cent of housing in Harlow and five per cent in Crawley were composed of flats. Many houses were terraced, with low-pitched roofs and open fronts, characteristic of American estates. However, most tenants would have preferred a private garden. New towns were later criticised for neglecting residents' needs, especially the insufficient emphasis given to essential communal facilities. This was particularly true of some large Glasgow estates where schools were slow to materialise.

A ground breaking 1957 study reviewed the extensive re-housing of inner-city tenants from London's Bethnal Green to Debden in Essex, twenty miles to the east. Michael Young and Peter Willmott's *Family and Kinship in East London* became a modern sociological classic. It examined the impact of moving tenants from old inner-city terraced homes to blocks of flats, or 'up to date semis' with small gardens. The benefits of modernisation had to be balanced against the loss of community feeling, which became more evident as slum re-housing progressed. Young and Willmott concluded that architects and planners had underestimated the social upheaval caused by such a dramatic lifestyle change. Their findings were disputed in later research which argued that the majority of tenants were just relieved to escape from insanitary slum housing.

The Lawn, Harlow (architect Frederick Gibberd), Britain's first residential high-rise received a 1956 Housing Award, with Grade II listing, 1998.

Crawley New Town's main architect was A. G. Sheppard Fidler, who also worked with Herbert Manzoni on Birmingham's 1950s comprehensive re-housing scheme. (Getty Images)

Rockingham Way in Stevenage New Town, 1956, provided local amenities including shops, pub and public transport. Few residents owned cars.

Alongside the enormous council building expansion of the 1950s, private housing continued to expand but at a relatively lower level until the consumer boom took hold later in the decade. Private ownership only increased when standards of living rose and mortgages became both more available and affordable.

4
Changing Interiors

Home interiors and furnishings underwent a fundamental change during the later 1950s. Full employment meant households had more disposable income. New technological aids for the home appeared, gradually becoming more affordable for the average householder. The development of combined living areas in newer homes led to interior spaces being used more efficiently. Indoor plumbing, formerly a luxury, began to be installed in many homes by the close of the decade.

Inside 1950s homes, the darker, heavier pre-war look and plain styles were gradually replaced by rooms emphasising colour and light. Modern interior design was given a boost by the Festival of Britain. Designers like Terence Conran and Robin Day showcased modern, light furniture. Modern chairs were evident throughout the site and Day notably produced tip-up seating for the new Festival Hall. The Antelope chair designed by Ernest Race was both unusual and successful. With its steel wire design, wavy arms and angled back, it was described as having 'Form, Wit, and Grace'.

Above: Ernest Race's Antelope chair, with its modern tubular design, was a huge success among many Festival of Britain visitors.
Right: A 1950s booklet on house cleaning targeted 'housewives'. It was a free gift with the 1950s magazine *Home Chat*.

How To Clean Everything About the House

By
Olive E. Ivory

Presented with 'Home Chat'

Did you know?

In 1951, furniture designer Robin Day's original teak and plywood stacking chair, the Hillestak, received accolades. A subsequent version, his famous polypropylene stacking chair, was later used in millions of church and village halls across Britain. Similar styles were still in use in 2016.

Replicating some of these high-end designs for a mass market was challenging and revealed a wide gulf between design and manufacture. Designers argued manufacturers ignored quality in their eagerness to reproduce 'modern' styles, while high street manufacturers criticised designers who only catered for an elite. High street copies sometimes had little in common with original designs, provoking derision from designers. 'Popular chairs with balls at the ends' was one scornful description of imitations of Race's Antelope chair, which, it was said, only purported to look functional.

From 1950, most homes had a guaranteed regular, dependable, electricity supply. Post-war power cuts were less frequent and reliable electricity encouraged consumers to purchase more appliances, especially once standardised ring mains and sockets became a legal requirement. Plug-in electric heaters made heating a practicality for upstairs rooms

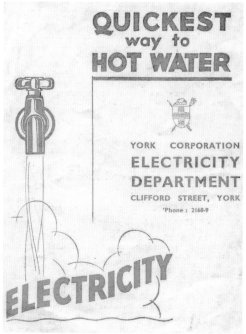

Above left: Gas Council 'convector radiant fire' advertisement. 'Mr Therm' and the black cat became an instantly recognisable 1950s Gas Council logo. (National Grid/Centrica)
Above right: Electricity was becoming more popular than gas. York Electricity Board advertised the merits of instant hot water in bathrooms and kitchens. (Northern Power Grid)

and the rapidly growing popularity of electric irons, and ironing boards, led to an extensive installation of electric sockets. Steep peaks in electricity usage were evident mornings and evenings, and on ironing days, usually Mondays or Tuesdays. Newly formed and more efficient local Gas and Electricity Boards competed for customers. However, it was 1960 before electrification reached the most remote rural areas.

Right: Heating in Felixstowe College student accommodation included an open fire, a 'plug-in' electric fire and modern central heating radiators. (Janet Shepherd)
Below: Student's bedroom/study, University of Bristol, 1953. A modern gas fire sits under a heavy, old-fashioned wooden fire surround. (Ken Parry)

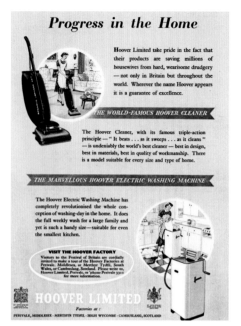

Progress in the Home

Hoover Limited take pride in the fact that their products are saving millions of housewives from hard, wearisome drudgery — not only in Britain but throughout the world. Wherever the name Hoover appears it is a guarantee of excellence.

THE WORLD-FAMOUS HOOVER CLEANER

The Hoover Cleaner, with its famous triple-action principle — "It beats ... as it sweeps ... as it cleans" — is undeniably the world's best cleaner — best in design, best in materials, best in quality of workmanship. There is a model suitable for every size and type of home.

THE MARVELLOUS HOOVER ELECTRIC WASHING MACHINE

The Hoover Electric Washing Machine has completely revolutionised the whole conception of washing-day in the home. It does the full weekly wash for a large family and yet is such a handy size—suitable for even the smallest kitchen.

VISIT THE HOOVER FACTORY
Visitors to the Festival of Britain are cordially invited to make a tour of the Hoover Factories at Perivale, Middlesex, or Merthyr Tydfil, South Wales, or Cambuslang, Scotland. Please write to, Hoover Limited, Perivale, or 'phone Perivale 3311 for more information.

HOOVER LIMITED
Factories at :
PERIVALE, MIDDLESEX · MERTHYR TYDFIL · HIGH WYCOMBE · CAMBUSLANG, SCOTLAND

A Hoover washing machine advertisement in 1951. Hoover, whose name was already synonymous with vacuum cleaners, was beginning to diversify. (Hoover)

From 1956, there had been a vast improvement in air quality, which benefited all city dwellers. After decades of pollution from coal fires, which often led to 'London Smogs' – most notably the 'Great Smog' of 1952, which caused 4,000 deaths – the Clean Air Act brought an end to severe pollution by creating zones where only smokeless fuel could be burned. With fewer open fires and more reliable electricity, homes became cleaner.

After the Second World War, men returned home to a peacetime economy. Women's roles changed as they were encouraged to embrace domesticity as housewives and mothers, although they also found part-time employment in factories and offices. Many of these changes in society were reflected in the 1950s home. In many households, it was the kitchen that altered most, changing across the decade from a scullery to an important place at the 'heart of the home'. It began to assume greater importance, described in a 1950 *Woman's Own* editorial as, 'the room more than any other you love to keep shining and bright. A woman's place? Yes, it is! For it is the heart and centre of the meaning of the home.'

In 1944, the Dudley Report listed kitchen necessities as a sink, draining board, working surface, ventilated larder, and cupboards. Ten years later, as consumerism took hold, the most sought-after kitchen goods were refrigerators, washing machines, electric cookers and stainless steel sinks.

Perhaps the most startling sight at the Festival of Britain was the use of bright colours, like lime yellow and bright green, with 'splashes of scarlet on the chair seats'. New chemicals led to colourful paints and bold textiles becoming easily available. Colour technology was incorporated into household plastics, heralding the start of popular laminated plastic worktops, soon known by the leading brand's name, 'Formica', with surfaces that could not be 'burned, scratched or stained'. Notable specialist firms like Hygena and Finch offered modern, efficient, colourful kitchens, incorporating all the latest technology. Probably the most sought-after kitchen gadget that appeared after the war was the modern pressure cooker, made of aluminium and stainless steel. It was very economical to use, as it drastically cut cooking times and also had separate containers, so several foods could be cooked together. Many 'baby boomers' remember homemade steamed puddings made in the pressure cooker in a third of the time needed for traditional steaming. The introduction of fluorescent lighting helped to improve working conditions and Venetian blinds appeared on kitchen windows, seen as very modern and easy to keep clean. As the market expanded, kitchen equipment became cheaper, although, for many households, large items like washing machines remained prohibitively expensive. Despite the desire to end daily shopping by owning a refrigerator, by 1959 only 13 per cent of British homes possessed one.

Right: In the 1950s, the leading brand Formica developed long-lasting, laminated kitchen countertops with colourful, popular 'wipe clean' surfaces. (Courtesy of Formica Group)
Below: A solid pink Formica topped table and chairs, purchased in Golders Green in 1954 and still in use in 2016. (Janet Shepherd)

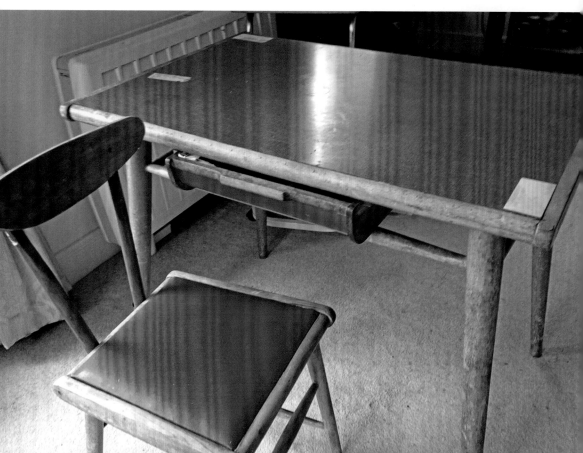

Colourful, modern, Hygena kitchen with a dividing unit and laminated worktops, displaying an electric food mixer and toaster. 1956. (Sainsbury's)

In 1946, visitors who had queued to see the *Britain Can Make It* exhibition were often more interested in displays of affordable small items for the home than the larger exhibits. This was much the same in the early 1950s, when a plethora of smaller attractive household items, especially china, came onto the market. The British pottery industry was undergoing highly significant changes, which reflected the optimism evident in British life in general as the decade progressed. Plain, white china was replaced by bright patterns and shapes as the British public shunned bland utility ware in favour of anything with colour. The Coronation of Queen Elizabeth II in 1953 provided opportunities for the pottery industry to produce attractive commemorative china, albeit in mainly traditional designs. Influences from the Festival of Britain permeated the industry and bright patterned crockery became especially popular, with ceramic designs displaying everyday life, holidays and abstract images. Designers assumed a far greater significance in the post-war years than had previously been the case. Well-known Stoke-on-Trent firms, such as Meakin and Midwinter, employed creative designers like Terence Conran and Jessie Tait. Midwinter produced innovative tableware in the 1950s, chiefly because it hired such top-class stylists. Meakin's reasonable prices and good design secured the firm a universal appeal. The classic Wedgwood firm, a market leader, opened outlets in major retail stores. There was some antipathy and lingering insularity on the part of some firms towards foreign designs but it was soon clear that Britain needed to produce ceramics that could compete in the most important export market, North America. Similarly, in the British home market, North American influences were beginning to flourish and, subsequently, some British firms started producing designs specifically for the USA.

Pallisey's hugely successful 'Regatta' pattern china featured seagulls and a yacht at sea, using an on-glaze silk-screen decoration method. (Janet Shepherd)

Alfred Meakin's 1950s French Boulevard design. Meakin produced a range of patterns for the export market, specifically targeting North American consumers. (Janet Shepherd)

Popular Stylecraft plate, designed by Jessie Tait for the Staffordshire pottery firm Midwinter. They produced quality earthernware and also stoneware. (Janet Shepherd)

By the mid-1950s, furnishings were less elaborate. Slimmer style furniture, often with metal legs and plywood frames, suited modern, smaller, homes. It was the age of 'thin legged coffee tables'. Fashionable and expensive designer styles, produced by elite companies like Hille & Race, were promoted in Ideal Home exhibitions, and in magazines like *House & Garden*, but only stocked in a limited number of high-end retailers like Heals. The well-known furniture designer, Gordon Russell, produced many pioneering designs across the decade – from light utility furniture to chairs for Basil Spence's re-built Coventry Cathedral.

The creation of new homes in the 1950s, with their smaller rooms and more open aspects, generally encouraged the purchase of less bulky furniture. Nonetheless, many British people found modern designs difficult to accept and there remained a sizeable demand for highly polished and decorative Art Deco pre-war styles. A visitor to Harlow New Town observed that

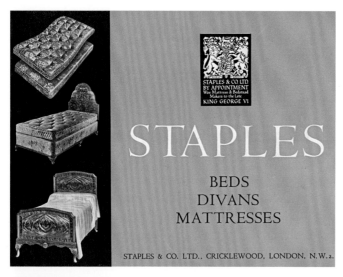

1950s Staples Beds booklet. Modern low divans with spring mattresses and sofa beds gradually replaced old-style iron bedsteads. (Staples Beds)

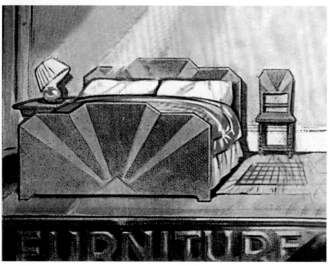

1950s postcard showing a modern double bed with a popular sun-ray design on the headboard, often also seen on garages. (Janet Shepherd)

Up-market, high-quality, stainless steel 1950s Sipelia fish cutlery. Sipelia were a well-known cutlery firm based in Sheffield. (Janet Shepherd)

the rooms were very small and filled with clumsy, oversized three-piece suites and unsuitable furniture such as large sideboards.

Class differences were noticeable. High-end furniture was not readily embraced by lower socio-economic groups, who often disliked, and could not afford, modern designs. The 1953 Ideal Home Exhibition's open-plan sitting and dining room proved unpopular with many visitors. In the same year, a Mass Observation Survey exhibition at Charing Cross station, *Register Your Choice*, revealed that a majority of consumers wanted comfort rather than style. Popular designs for lounge furniture in the Festival of Britain's Lansbury Estate included 'homely and British' three-piece suites, with a settee and two individual chairs. Gender differences were apparent: there was a larger chair for a man and a smaller one for a woman with 'firm support for the back and ample elbow room for sewing and knitting'. Among the middle classes, the aspirational nouveau riche often emulated the declining upper classes, purchasing items they considered to be in the 'best possible taste'. Poet John Betjeman mocked such pretentiousness in 'How to Get On In Society' (1958), which begins, 'Phone for the fish knives, Norman'.

Did you know?

Coronation chicken was the decade's most famous dish, created for the Coronation of Queen Elizabeth 11 in 1953. When rationing ended, chicken became more widely available. By mid-decade, Bird's Eye was selling the first frozen chicken pies. Foreign foods became popular and 'chicken chop suey and chips' appeared on holiday camp menus.

From mid-decade, the impact of television was immense. Following a rapid surge for the Coronation, by 1956 nearly half of all households had a black-and-white television; colour did not arrive until the mid-1960s. Most sets were rented for a few shillings a week, often a cheaper option than an outright purchase. By the close of the decade, television became the focal point in many living rooms alongside the radio, or wireless, both often proudly displayed in polished wooden cabinets. The expansion of new housing fed the demand for smaller,

Above: A large Marconi radio, bought in Bruce Grove, Tottenham, in the mid 1950s and still in daily use in 2016. (Pete Mulvey)

Below left: 'Brighten your home'. Berger's new paint, 'Brolac', was advertised as very suitable for steamy atmospheres in kitchens and bathrooms. (Crown Paints Ltd)

'You're so handsome
...and a genius too!'

'Thank you, Jane. These colours really are rather good.'
'You're putting it on so smoothly!'
'I'm a smooth character . . . . but seriously, Brolac is the easiest paint I've ever used. It covers the old paint so well.'
'It's absolutely gorgeous, John darling. The Browns are going to be green with envy.'
'Another thought has just occurred to me, Jane.'
'What's that, my clever decorator-husband?'
'With this quality paint it won't need doing again for a long time, will it?'
'We'll see about that, my sweet.'

**BRIGHTEN YOUR HOME WITH
BROLAC AND MURAC P·E·P**

lighter, more versatile furniture. The use of light woods, plus the arrival of fitted carpets later in the decade, made rooms seem larger, brighter and warmer. Discerning customers with money to spend chose furniture produced by newer firms like Ercol and G Plan. Ercol had gained some success with a modern version of the traditional Windsor chair, but generally had limited public appeal. More successful G-Plan arrived in 1953, with its wider range of pale oak furniture. G-Plan became popular for several reasons. The use of light oak was regarded as stylish and modern. Furthermore, the firm's effectiveness lay in its marketing; it bypassed retailers and advertised straight to customers in glossy magazines. G-Plan also produced the first range of furniture in Britain that could be bought piece by piece. By continuing to produce the same ranges over several years, the firm enabled budget-conscious customers to add matching furniture at a later date. Nevertheless, higher prices meant the firm still only reached a small percentage of the furniture market.

Colour and contrast became the key to the success of much modern interior design. Three plain living room walls were often complimented with a brightly coloured fourth. Top fabric designers like Jacqueline Groag, Marianne Mahler, and Lucienne Day focused on bold colours and abstract patterns for

Above left: Marley tiles, the 'modern way to stop draughts, impervious to decay and dry rot, stainproof, easy to clean'. 1955. (With permission of the Marley Tile Company Ltd)

Above right: 'Make your house a home'. Crown wallpaper advertisement, showing five of their most popular designs for modern wallpaper, 1955. (Reproduced by kind permission of CWV Wallcoverings Ltd, the registered owners of the Crown trademark for wallpaper)

the top end of the market. Some new abstract styles were successfully adapted by high street firms, both for their intrinsic design and, increasingly, as a fashion statement. Nevertheless, there were still many manufacturers meeting a continuing demand for traditional styles, like Regency stripes and floral wallpaper.

There were still millions of households, however, who were unable to afford any modernisation or new technology, and were trapped in old, decaying accommodation. Multiple occupancy and large families were forced to exist in cramped conditions. In particular, it was the lack of efficient or even adequate plumbing that made life arduous for so many households. In 1950, approximately 10 million people were living in homes 'without a hot water system, indoor lavatory or fixed bath'. For many families, tin baths in front of living room fireplaces, and shared outside toilets were the norm. Some grants were available for the installation of bathrooms but by 1954 only 10,000 had been installed. By 1959, it was mandatory for all local authorities to provide grants for homeowners who were prepared to install a fixed bath, a wash basin, an indoor toilet (usually in a separate room adjacent to the bathroom) plus hot and cold running water. 80,000 bathroom installations were approved and, by 1960, the housing minister was able to report a huge countrywide improvement: 'a mother at last has got a proper bath with hot water from the tap in which to bath the children instead of a tin bath on the floor with water from the kettle'. By the end of the 1950s, indoor plumbing was transforming the lives of ordinary people.

5
The New Consumers

In 1957, a foreign view of Britain's housing progress was provided by *New York Times* journalist Drew Middleton. He described the new British working man moving 'to a New Town or a housing estate from a slum or near slum ... He is living in what is to him comparative luxury: a living room, a clean and, by British standards, modern kitchen. There is a bedroom for the children and a modern bath and toilet'.

Middleton rightly drew attention to improvements in living conditions by the later 1950s. A boom in Western economies and an annual growth rate of 2 to 3 per cent produced relative affluence, virtual full employment, and a growth in disposable income. In 1955, Mary Quant's fashion world arrived, helped by a new phenomenon: the 'teenager', keen to spend spare money on clothes, magazines, cosmetics and music. For the first time, there appeared a demonstrable link between adolescence and consumerism.

In 1956, two London exhibitions featured possible future housing trends. *This Is Tomorrow*, a multi-disciplinary art exhibition at London's Whitechapel Art Gallery, included a room with a strawberry-perfumed carpet. The whole exhibition was the result of a unique collaboration between architects, painters, sculptors and other artists. At the Daily Mail Ideal Home Exhibition, which acted as a shop window for up-to-date ideas, a million visitors visited the star exhibit, the 'House of the Future', designed by architects Alison and Peter Smithson. This ultra-modern one-bedroom futuristic '1980' town house included an internal patio garden and a coffee table that rose from the floor at the press of a button. The roof was covered in aluminium foil to reflect the sun's rays. Almost everything in the house was made of plastic, the latest popular material. The house itself was air-conditioned and warmed by underfloor heating with a short-wave transmitter containing push buttons to control the electronic equipment. Dubbed 'science fiction', it bore little relation to most people's lives and was generally disliked by the public.

Entrance to Westwood House flats, Woodberry Down, 2016. The lift and stairs remain unchanged since the 1950s, including original name plates. (John Shepherd)

Despite the money expended on council estates and new towns, much housing remained poor. While some families began to have disposable cash for the first time, others were living hand to mouth. In major cities like London, Sheffield, Manchester and Birmingham, people were still housed in cramped, damp, draughty Victorian terraces. In 1958, sociologist Peter Townsend estimated there were 7 million people still living in poverty. Only a fifth of the population were living in houses built to standards set fourteen years earlier by the Dudley Committee. Greater subsidies for flats following the 1956 Housing Act resulted in higher and higher tower blocks appearing across the country.

For others, however, life in the later 1950s began to be about more than just working to survive. There was increased leisure time to enjoy at home. Consumers sought modernity and, by the end of the decade, most households had something 'up-to-the-minute', either large or small kitchen items or newly installed indoor bathrooms and toilets.

1955 saw the arrival of Independent Television (ITV). Sponsored by advertising, it led to a large growth in consumer spending.

Did you know?

Independent Television's launch, September 23 1955, was overshadowed by the fictional death of *The Archers* radio star, Grace Archer. Arguably, this was a deliberate plan by the BBC to sabotage ITV's launch. Many of the public mourned Grace's death as if she had been a real person.

Television advertisements targeted shoppers in a way previously unknown, coming directly into their living rooms. Manufacturers and retailers recognised that it was primarily women to whom they needed to appeal in order to sell their products. Television adverts urged them to purchase labour-saving products to improve their lifestyles.

Memorable advertisements from the later 1950s included Rice Krispies' *Snap Crackle & Pop* and Rowntrees' *Don't forget the Fruit Gums Mum!* By the end of the decade, most of Britain was within range of both a BBC and ITV transmitter and the number of television licenses

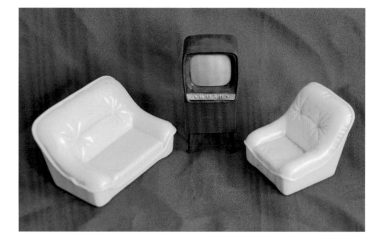

1950s dolls' house furniture: sofa, armchair and a television. Real objects and designs are often replicated in dolls' house furnishings. (Janet Shepherd)

overtook radio. The arrival of television brought home entertainment into a new era, while visits to the cinema declined. In 1952, the single television channel, the BBC, had closed down in national mourning following the death of George VI. By 1960, there were two channels, and 10 million television sets were in operation with half the population watching at peak times.

Did you know?

The last British radio programme to attract a larger evening audience than television was *Journey into Space*, a children's science fiction series set in futuristic 1965 when writer, Charles Chiltern, thought men would first walk on the moon. He was only four years too early.

Advertising also boosted the hire purchase (HP) market. Buying on the 'never-never' suited the aspirational mood of the later 1950s. Items were increasingly bought on credit, often with the 'tally man' calling each week for payment. The ending of HP restrictions in 1958 led to a surge in demand for cars, refrigerators, and furniture. By the late 1950s, half of all television sets and a third of vacuum cleaners were bought through hire purchase. More money was also spent on gambling, especially horse racing, greyhound racing and football pools. Watching football was an important part of working-class life. Matches were regularly played on Saturdays, with a 3 p.m. kick-off, when most people had time away from work. The FA Cup Final was a very popular annual event. Throughout the 1950s, weekly betting on football results was a family activity, with one in three Britons trying to win money on 'the pools' from firms like Vernons and Littlewoods.

The post-war shortage of labour meant that tradesmen were expensive and in short supply. This, together with an increase of leisure time led to an upsurge in DIY from the mid-1950s, with these years sometimes referred to as the 'decade of DIY'. A thrifty generation, who had grown very familiar with 'make do and mend' during the war years, took very readily to the new DIY craze. New chemicals formed the basis of specialist products for the home enthusiast, including emulsion paint, rollers, and a wider range of wallpapers, helped by easy-mix wall paper paste – all of which increased the popularity of DIY. Polycell's range of adhesives and fillers, notably 'Polyfilla', appeared. ICI brought out their successful Dulux

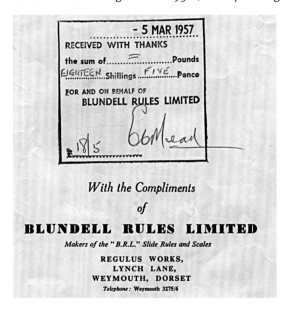

With the Compliments

of

BLUNDELL RULES LIMITED

Makers of the " B.R.L." Slide Rules and Scales

REGULUS WORKS,
LYNCH LANE,
WEYMOUTH, DORSET

Telephone : Weymouth 3275/6

DIY expert Barry Bucknell advocated precise measuring instruments. To aid post-war employment, some firms like Blundell Rules received a government contract. (Janet Shepherd)

paint in 1953 and DIY enthusiasts were soon enamoured of the new light paints that began to flood the market, replacing the old favourite, 'dirt concealing brown'. A year later, Black & Decker moved into the domestic market and introduced what became their spectacularly famous electric drill. Black & Decker's successful advertising campaign resulted in a massive increase in sales. In 1955, the monthly women's magazine *Pins and Needles Plus Home-Making* declared that

> everywhere you look, today, there is evidence of the tremendous 'do it yourself' boom that has started to make Britain's home-owners into a new generation of weekend carpenters and decorators ... There isn't a room in the house that will not offer us some chance for improvement at a modest outlay, so let's become spare-time craftsmen in repairing, enlarging, modernising and cabinet making.

For many, DIY was synonymous with the popular *Barry Bucknell's Do It Yourself* BBC television programmes, which included demonstrations on how to update older properties by boxing in Victorian fireplaces or covering panelled doors with plywood. Numerous interested visitors attended the first national DIY exhibition held at Olympia in 1956. Specialist DIY magazines boomed, providing detailed help for the amateur. Pages of advertisements for the latest products and techniques demonstrated, for example, how to build a fitted kitchen. One edition of the *Practical Householder* even advertised an 'architect designed' bungalow that cost £2,000 but could apparently be built by a DIY enthusiast for under £1,000. *Practical Householder* for

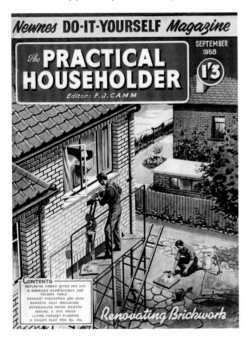 

Above left: *Practical Householder* became the best-selling monthly DIY 1950s magazine, with articles on house renovations, furniture construction, laying flooring etc.
Above right: *The Home Handyman* also provided detailed instructions on home improvements and, like *Practical Householder*, it almost exclusively targeted men.

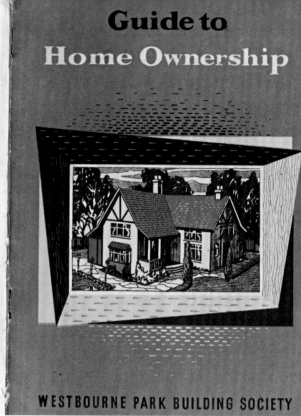

Guide to Home Ownership

WESTBOURNE PARK BUILDING SOCIETY

Above: The Baptist Church's Westbourne Park Building Society's home ownership guide in the late 1950s encouraged customers to take out mortgages. (Britannia Building Society)

Below left: Scottish Legal, Glasgow, advertised mortgage or cash deals for house purchases and promoted endowment mortgages during a low inflation period. 1958 booklet. (Reproduced with kind permission from Scottish Friendly Assurance Society)

September 1958 had over twenty-four pages of adverts followed by a variety of diverse articles by different experts, even including one on how to build your own spin drier to complement the latest washing machines on the market.

By the late 1950s, and with full employment, a 'property owning democracy', encouraged by successive Conservative governments, began to thrive. Increased consumer confidence was reflected in home investment and a growing demand for mortgages. Stamp duty, payable on the sale of properties over a certain price, was reduced, resulting in more building society mortgages becoming available. More homes were privately owned, rising from 29 per cent in 1951 to 45 per cent by the early 1960s.

Holidays, notably at Britain's seaside resorts, became more affordable. Many families stayed in the cheaper bed-and-breakfast accommodation where they had to vacate their rooms after breakfast and were not permitted to return until the evening. Coastal holiday camps thrived in the 1950s, notably Butlins and Pontins, where plentiful food and reasonable prices attracted a large number of holidaymakers. Caravanning was a further leisure activity that had increased in popularity by the end of the decade, owing mainly to the surge in car ownership. The new arrival was the package holiday, dubbed 'Travel Off the Peg'. By 1958, charter flights transported 2 million tourists, mainly middle-class, abroad for an annual break.

Cultural influences emanating from the United States, which became known as 'Americanisation', expanded in the later 1950s. Many Britons, particularly teenagers, were increasingly drawn to all things American – films, foods, clothing (especially jeans), life styles and desirable labour-saving gadgets. 1959 saw the arrival in Britain of American 'house to house selling' cosmetics firm, Avon, with its catch phrase, 'Avon Calling!' Features seen in open-plan Californian houses began to be replicated in some quality modern British one-storey bungalows, bringing a wider range of materials, colour and texture with a combination of steel, brick, glass and concrete. These American influences were especially noticeable in the use of larger windows, which in turn let more light into the home. Large estates with privately built rows of neat bungalows, popular in the inter-war years, mushroomed again from the late 1950s. They typified post-war middle-class suburbia, particularly in coastal areas like the Wirral in Cheshire. The annual Daily Mail Ideal Home Exhibition produced many useful books for would-be homeowners,

A colourful late-1950s traycloth. With more disposable income, families travelled to the seaside for day trips and holidays. The most sought-after resorts were Brighton in the south and Blackpool in the north. (Janet Shepherd)

'For health and happiness bring your family to Butlins this summer'. Holiday camps increasingly attracted families during the 1950s. (Courtesy of Butlins Heritage Collection)

Late-1950s advertisement enticing people to holiday 'abroad' in the Isle of Man, showing Douglas Bay harbour and ferry.

including the *Daily Mail Book of Bungalow Plans* for those 'looking for a bungalow to suit their needs'. Bungalows were becoming the 'must-have' retirement house by the later 1950s. Bungalow plans in the 1958 *Daily Mail* book included an open-plan kitchen 'on the American plan' with fitted cupboards that reached the ceiling, a 12-foot-wide Formica worktop and a stainless steel sink. Bungalows were also reproduced in children's toys. The toy firm, Louis Marx & Co., established in a post-war housing estate in Swansea to provide much needed local employment, produced a range of colourful and popular toy tin bungalows.

As the economy recovered, there was a greater demand from higher income families for architect-designed homes, which were often large, open-plan houses with enormous picture windows. Trevor Dannart, an important British Modernist architect who had studied under modernist Peter Moro and had worked on the Royal Festival Hall, designed an ultra-modern, unique house in Cambridge in the late 1950s. His state-of-the-art, five-bedroom house was built for the historian and political scientist Professor Peter Laslett. It was particularly noted for its long open-plan living room and enormous fireplace. Also in Cambridge, a quality modern private estate of flats and houses, Highsett, arose in the late 1950s, designed by Eric Lyons, Geoffrey Townsend, and their architectural and property development company, Span. Low blocks of open-plan flats, maisonettes and garages were grouped in a university-style collegiate quadrangle, where the modernist design was tempered by the liberal use of brick. Span's radical designs attempted to combine a modern approach with a close attention to

A large, detached, traditionally designed and privately built 1950s Herefordshire brick dwelling with a very large garden. Photograph 2016. (Janet Shepherd)

A 1950s postcard showing semi-detached bungalows with neat front gardens. There are only three cars in Martins Avenue, Denmead, Hampshire. (Ben Brooksbank)

detail. Lyons and Townsend shared a vision of good housing: 'not whether it can be built easily but whether it can be lived in easily'. They always sought to harmonise their homes with the environment. Their house designs usually had mono-pitch roofs with large, high-level windows and open-plan interiors. Landscaping was always high on Span's agenda with the inclusion of carefully landscaped gardens. At Highsett, existing well-established trees were incorporated into communal gardens. Two later phases followed in the 1960s and in 1998 Highsett received Grade II listing.

Gardens became more important in both private and council homes as leisure time increased. As rationing disappeared, the need for allotments declined. A wider range of foods became available in the shops and many wartime 'Dig for Victory' vegetable plots were

Architect-designed Laslett House, Cambridge, 1958. This unique well-maintained house, listed by English Heritage in 2004, still looked ultra-modern in 2016. (Janet Shepherd)

In 1958, two models from Johnsons of Great Yarmouth stand on a very modern, open-plan staircase advertising sailcloth skirts.

Bayco was a popular model construction kit for children throughout the 1950s. It often advertised children building houses – here a large detached dwelling and separate garage. (Meccano)

turned into lawns and flower beds. Neat suburban houses with immaculate front gardens on public view became the goal for many.

However, in many households growing vegetables and fruit continued as a hobby or to help supplement the family budget. Small areas were frequently utilised at the bottom of the back garden, often out of sight behind a tall hedge. Potatoes, carrots, runner beans and soft fruit were commonly grown. A 1953 survey in Derby reported that gardening continued to be a popular weekend hobby among working class men. Articles on how to improve gardens and outside areas featured in DIY magazines. A 1958 article entitled 'Concrete in the Garden' showed readers how to make steps, crazy paving, a sundial, ponds and garden seats. A 1950s gardening diary included this entry for 4 June:

A really hot June day. Eve planted out 25 tomato plants and I staked same, I also cut and clipped, and rolled front and back lawns and re-edged same, and I also put Sweet Peas in back garden to stakes and tied up a really terrific Delphinium. Have caught sun on my back. Eve and I finished re-decorating the bathroom. Very satisfactory and quick job.

43–45 Hills Road, Cambridge, just prior to demolition before the construction of the modern Span estate, Highsett. Photograph, 1957. (Cambridgeshire Collection)

The first phase of Span's Highsett estate in Cambridge in the late 1950s comprised thirty-one flats, maisonettes and garages on a prime city site. Photograph 2016. (Janet Shepherd)

The *New Statesman* journalist Geoffrey Goodman commented in 1956 on 'the bright bricks of new homes, hedged with well-tended gardens'. By the end of the decade, over three-fifths of houses possessed a garden.

Above all, as Britain prospered, the car became the symbol of status and affluence, ideally housed in a garage alongside the clipped front lawn. Car sales received an early boost in 1950 with the end of petrol rationing, although initially motorbikes and sidecars proved popular and cheaper alternatives, as did cycling, with many people joining cycling clubs. Car ownership doubled in the 1950s, with 3 million cars on Britain's roads by 1955, rising to around 6 million by 1960. Top-selling 1950s family cars included the Standard Vanguard, which was styled to resemble a 'scaled down American car'. It was initially intended for export but was seen on British roads in large numbers in the 1950s. Vauxhall Cresta was a bigger saloon car with American-style chrome and wide comfortable bench seats. The Morris Minor was one of the decade's most-loved cars and was the first British car to sell 1 million models in 1959. Two 'baby' Ford cars, the Ford Anglia and Ford Popular, were often produced in bright 'Festival-of-Britain colours'.

Car owners recognised that garaging their cars in a secure, weatherproof building would help prevent rust and keep it in good condition. Garages provided both protection from the vagaries of the British climate and from possible thieves. Home garages, frequently wooden with corrugated asbestos roof sheeting, were increasingly in demand. A 1950s advertising leaflet from C. & R. Constructions Ltd featured different garage designs.

Above left: Post-war, the number of allotment holders declined. However, growing vegetables at home was a common pastime, helping some families supplement the weekly budget. (Janet Shepherd)
Above right: Gardens with bright colourful flower beds became increasingly popular as the decade progressed, particularly in more prosperous middle-class households. (Janet Shepherd)

Several had decorative lathes fitted above the doors in a 'rising sun' design that became very typical of post-war domestic garage buildings. In 1957, the most sought-after garages, for those prepared to pay £20, boasted revolutionary sliding 'up and over' doors – a 'marvel to behold'.

Overall, the nation had more disposable cash, and the government regularly urged people to save patriotically by investing in tax-free National Savings. In 1956, a new way to save, and perhaps make a profit, came with the introduction of Premium Bonds. The bonds were brought in by the Chancellor of the Exchequer, Harold Macmillan, who unveiled them in his 1956 April budget as 'something completely new for the saver'. At a time of low inflation, 'no-one could lose' and there was always a chance of winning the top prize of £1,000. Winning numbers were chosen randomly by an Electronic Random Number Indicator Equipment machine, ERNIE for short, erroneously thought to be named after Ernest Marples, the Conservative MP who had implemented the scheme. Geoffrey Fisher, the Archbishop of Canterbury, disapproved, regarding bonds as a form of gambling rather than saving. However, Harold Macmillan was probably more in tune with public thinking. The scheme was generally well received because, unlike most lotteries and in the years before rising inflation, Premium Bonds guaranteed the investor's capital. Janet's mother bought one of the first bonds, convinced she would win. She never did and the bond still remained in the draw in 2016. By then, more than a third of the national population were still 'investing' in Premium Bonds.

Thorn & Sons, of Lancashire and Kent, advertised a range of home garage designs in concrete and also asbestos. 1957.

Eric and Nora Phillips proudly reveal their newly cleaned first car, a Standard Vanguard. Outside their Llanelli home, 1955. (Christine Parry)

Above left: Numerous 1950s posters urged the public to save securely with National Savings Certificates. Here a family views a desirable bungalow. (The National Archives)

Above right: Government-inspired Premium Bonds began in 1956 to encourage more saving. This advertisement announced the first draw, 1 June 1957.

Right: Kenwood Chef mixer, 1956. It was described as 'today's kitchen staff', an historic reference to the pre-First World War world of servants. (With kind permission of © Kenwood Ltd)

6
The 1950s Legacy

The years between 1950 and 1959 witnessed an overall improvement in living standards and an unprecedented rise in consumerism. By the close of the decade, the spotlight had moved from planners to consumers. Full employment resulted in more disposable income to spend during increased leisure time, as wages doubled and new goods became affordable, often purchased through HP. An affluent teenage market noticeably boosted consumer growth. By 1958, nearly a third of British households owned a car. Daily trips to local shops were replaced by weekly car journeys to the new supermarkets. It was a far cry from trams, trolleybuses and horse-drawn milk and coal floats, all still commonly seen in 1950. Commuting from ever-expanding suburbs to employment in the cities became a regular part of life for many. 'Let us be frank about it, most of our people have never had it so good', Prime Minister Harold MacMillan famously said in 1957 as the 'buy buy buy' mantra evolved.

Throughout this changing decade, politicians, architects and planners significantly influenced housing design and construction. Blitzed buildings and slums gradually disappeared from the landscape. Public housing dominated as 2.5 million people were rehoused in council estates of low- and high-rise homes, and into new towns. As the overall standard of living rose, home ownership expanded and the number of private houses increased.

Did you know?

In many households increased leisure allowed more time for reading. Boots the Chemist ran a private lending library throughout the 1950s. For a small charge, books could be borrowed and returned to any branch that displayed a Boots Green Shield sign.

More disposable income meant that people began to eat out more. 2016 copy of Wimpy's late 1950s famous trademark plastic tomato sauce bottle. (Janet Shepherd)

A 1950s, detached, well-maintained private house in a leafy Cambridge suburb was on the market in 2016 for £1.3 million. (Janet Shepherd)

Homes were brighter, cleaner and more comfortable. Interior plumbing with hot water, fitted baths and indoor toilets transformed lives. The spread of electricity and technological advances led to an unprecedented labour-saving era, while the luxury of central heating began to be installed in new homes. For the first time, some working-class households could replace linoleum flooring with fitted carpets. Changing patterns of consumption saw old staples like sugar lumps and rabbit disappear, being replaced by sliced bread and frozen foods. In 1957, the launch of *Which?*, the consumer magazine, was a response to the popular demand of consumerism. Large items like cars, washing machines or refrigerators, started to be specifically designed for short, disposable lives as the concept of obsolescence grew.

Did you know?

In 2016, a refrigerator belonging to the late Queen Mother – still standing in the Castle of Mey kitchen, Caithness – passed its annual electricity check. It was made in 1954, a surprising example of 1950s longevity.

The legacy of 1950s housing overwhelmingly came from the public sector, with council housing accounting for roughly half of all homes built after the Second World War. Tower blocks multiplied from the late 1950s, but the earlier utopian vision of 'streets in the sky', promoted by idealistic architects and planners, fell into disrepute. The detrimental effects associated with isolated living in high blocks gradually became apparent in the later 1960s. This was especially true for children, where living high up, with no easy access to gardens and playgrounds, denied them the freedom to play outside. Furthermore, high blocks were often found to have construction faults, necessitating expensive maintenance. Fundamental flaws in Ronan Point, a twenty-two-storey East London block, led to its collapse in 1968, in which four people died. Public disaffection escalated.

1950s high-rise blocks, however, were still occupied in 2016, along with other 1950s homes: detached, semi-detached, terraced houses and bungalows. Many of these have been well maintained and modernised. 'Baby boomers' are moving to bungalows, often those built in the 1950s; with no stairs to contend with, one-storey living increasingly appeals. Surveys have revealed that bungalows retain their popularity and that, in the choice of a house's name, 'The Bungalow' is the third most popular for British homes, after 'The Cottage' and 'Rose Cottage'. Modern equivalents are hard to find: in 2009, across the country, only 300 new bungalows were built. Temporary prefabs, originally designed for a short life, are still occupied, with Bristol retaining an unprecedented 700 prefabricated homes across seventeen estates.

The rear view of one of the massive, concrete, centrally heated 'luxury' blocks on Woodberry Down estate. Photograph, 2016. (John Shepherd)

Above: A row of 1950s semi-detached council houses, updated and in good condition. Some are now privately owned following the 1980s 'right to buy' scheme. Photograph, 2016. (Janet Shepherd)

Right: 1950s pensioners' prefabs. They have lasted and also been updated with up-to-the-minute modern solar panels. Photograph, 2016. (Karen Livingstone)

For most people, the close of the 1950s brought improvements in living conditions far removed from the austerity experienced at the start of the decade. There was a greater conformity of standards between private and public housing. The 1950s saw a change in how people lived, moving from basic austerity after the war, with many families in slum housing, to comfortable homes with indoor plumbing, new technology and enough disposable income to enjoy the burgeoning consumer society. In 1961, the Parker Morris Report, *Homes for Today and Tomorrow*, looked to the future to ensure housing would match the continuing rise in living standards.

In November 2016, the government was considering new-style prefabs, termed 'modular homes', to help ease the current housing crisis; Terence Conran recalled the Festival of Britain, as he celebrated the re-booting of the Design Museum in West London and concrete became chic, with upmarket advertisements for concrete magazine racks, lamps and rocking chairs.

By the close of the decade, in a time of increasing affluence, more Britons had disposable cash to spend on cars and holidays. A full car park at Braid Hills Hotel, Edinburgh, late 1950s. (Janet Shepherd)

7
What Now?

Life in 1950s Britain, and the details of the 1950s home, have been well documented in books, magazines, and online, and there are a number of places to visit that give a particularly good idea of what domestic life was like during the decade. For those readers who wish to pursue an interest in 1950s design, there are societies that provide a useful starting point such as:

The Decorative Arts Society is concerned with the study and appreciation of all aspects of decorative art from the 1850s to the present day – it arranges study visits to different collections.
The Decorative Arts Society, PO Box 136, Woodbridge, Suffolk, IP12 1TG
www.decorativeartssociety.org.uk

The National Association of Decorative and Fine Arts Societies (NADFAS) has a network of 360 local societies across the country, which promote arts education, appreciation and preservation of our artistic heritage. They organise regular meetings, visits, tours etc.
NADFAS, 8, Guildford St, London, WC1N 1DA. Tel: 0207 430 0730.
www.nadfas.org.uk

The Twentieth Century Society is concerned with the safeguarding of twentieth-century architecture and design, and is especially interested in education and conservation. It organises lectures, tours, walks, etc.
The Twentieth Century Society, 70 Crowcross St, London, EC1M 6EJ. Tel: 0207 250 3857.
www.c2osociety.org.uk

Further Reading

1. Ferry, Kathryn, *The 1950s Kitchen* (Shire, 2011)
   The author explores 1950s designs for the domestic kitchen and its evolving importance as 'the heart of the home'.
2. Hanley, Lynsey, *Estates: An Intimate History* (Granta Books, 2008)
   Examines life on post-war British estates, through the author's own experiences in Birmingham and London.
3. Hennessey, Peter, *Having It So Good: Britain in the Fifties* (Allen Lane, 2006)
   A very readable history of the 1950s, from austerity to affluence, by one of Britain's foremost historians.
4. Kynaston, David, *Family Britain 1951–57* (Bloomsbury, 2010)
   A vivid and detailed portrait of British family life in the 1950s, with a diverse range of sources.
5. McClaren, Graham, *Ceramics of the 1950s* (Shire, 1997)
   Examines how pottery manufacturers met the challenge of a post-war world that demanded bright, modern, exciting ceramics.

6. Opie, Robert, *The 1950s Scrapbook* (New Cavendish Books, 1998)
   Large pictorial, evocative 1950s images, taken from the Robert Opie's Museum of Advertising & Packaging, Gloucester.
7. Shepherd, Janet and Shepherd, John, *1950s Childhood* (Shire, 2015)
   The authors recall growing up as part of the 'Baby Boomer' generation in post-war Britain.
8. Young, Michael and Willmott, Peter, *Family and Kinship in East London* (Penguin Books, 1980)
   The classic sociological 1957 study of extensive 1950s re-housing from London's Bethnal Green to Debden in Essex.
9. Addison, Paul, *Now The War Is Over: A Social History of Britain, 1945–51* (BBC, Jonathan Cape, 1985)
   Explores the society that demobilised troops returned to in 1945; see especially Chapter Three, 'A Home of our Own'. Enlarges on themes originally explored in a 1980s eight-part television series of the same name.
10. Worth, Jennifer, *Call The Midwife: A True Story of the East End in the 1950s* (Phoenix, 2012)
    Memoir of a London midwife working in the East End in the 1950s. The book was made into a popular television series, *Call The Midwife*, in 2012.

Places to Visit

1. The Design Museum, 224-238 High Street Kensington, London, W8 6AG. www.designmuseum.org. Tel: 0870 833 9955.
   One of the world's leading contemporary design museums. In November 2016 it moved to its new Kensington venue.
2. Geffrye Museum, 136 Kingsland Road, London, E2 8EA. www.geffrye-museum.org.uk. Tel: 0207 739 9893
   This 'Museum of the Home' displays a history of English homes from 1600 to the present day, with period homes and gardens.
3. Museum of Domestic Design and Architecture (MoDA), Middlesex University, 9 Bouvelard Drive, Beaufort Park, Colindale, London, NW9 5HF. moda@mdx.ac.uk. Tel: 0208 4115 244
   MoDA boasts a 'history of domestic interiors' with a notable collection of domestic design artefacts, including textiles, books, catalogues, magazines and a large range of Crown wallpapers.
4. Victoria and Albert Museum, Cromwell Road, London, SW7 2RL. www.vam.ac.uk. Tel: 0207942 2000.
   This internationally renowned museum has a large collection of 1950s paintings, crockery, artefacts and ephemera.
5. The Museum of Brands. www.museumofbrands.com. Tel: 0207 243 9611.
   Includes an extensive and varied collection of 1950s packaging and ephemera.
6. The Prefab Museum, 17 Meliot Road, Catford, London, SE6 1RY. www.prefabmuseum.uk. Tel: 0750 7068 710.
   The museum contains maps and information about prefabs still existing in Britain today; it also has 'open house' prefabs to visit.
7. Cae Dai 1950s Era Museum, Cae Dai Trust, Lawnt, Denbigh, N. Wales, LL16 4SU. caetrust@50smuseum.uk. Tel: 01745 817004.
   Contains 1950s rooms, shops and artefacts, with a large collection of televisions, radios, record players and cameras.

8. The Tenement House, 145 Buccleuch St, Glasgow, G3 6QN.
   www.nts.org.uk/ptoperty/tenement-house. Tel: 0141 3330183
   An untouched and preserved tenement flat lived in by Agnes Toward and her mother
   from 1911–65, which includes 1950s ephemera.
9. Cambridge & County Folk Museum, 2/3 Castle Street, Cambridge, CB3 0AO. www.
   folkmuseum.org.uk. Tel: 01223 355159.
   Exhibits centre on the everyday social life of the people of Cambridge. Features homes of
   the past including the 1950s.
10. Gordon Russell Museum, 15 Russell Square, Broadway, Worcestershire, W12 7AP. www.
    gordonrussellmuseum.org. Tel: 01386 854695.
    The museum is dedicated to the pioneering work of the twentieth-century furniture
    designer, Gordon Russell, and is situated in his original workshop. Shows a range of his
    work from Utility furniture to luxury modernist pieces.

Websites

General information, images and 1950s items can be sourced at **www.amazon.co.uk** and on
the image-collecting website **Pinterest** (see specifically https://uk.pinterest.com/1950sdecor)
and also on the **BBC Homes Design** site (http://www.bbc.co.uk/homes/design/period_1950s.
shtml).

Readers interested in collecting ceramics could usefully visit **www.keyesceramics.com**
where there is a range of information and help.

More specific websites for 1950s homes and housing include the following:
1. 'A History of Social Housing'. Brian Wheeler. BBC NEWS / 14 April 2015. http://www.bbc.
   co.uk/news/uk-14380936
   Examines housing in Britain, from 'Homes fit for Heroes' after the First World War to the
   1980s 'property owning democracy'.
2. 'Homes Through the Decades: The Making of Modern Housing'. NHBC Home. 26 March
   2015. http://www.nhbc.co.uk/NewsandComment/Documents/filedownload,59849,en.pdf
   Images and information about changes in British housing, from Victorian times into the
   twenty-first century. National House Building Council (NHBC).
3. The Park Hill Estate, Sheffield: 'Streets in the Sky'. Municipal Dreams. https://municipaldreams.
   wordpress.com/2013/04/16/the-park-hill-estate-sheffield-streets-in-the-sky/
   Page about Sheffield's enormous 1957 Park Hill high-rise estate. There is also a BBC
   documentary on this subject, presented by Tom Dyckhoff – *Saving Britain's Past – Streets
   in the Sky – Park Hill*, which is available on YouTube.
4. Absolutely prefabulous: 'Residents of Britain's last prefab estate battle to save homes
   built to last only ten years'. *Daily Mail*. Article 1347259. 15 January 2011. http://www.
   dailymail.co.uk/news/article-1347259/Britains-prefab-estate-residents-battle-save-homes-
   built-10-years-ago.html
   Robert Hardman's *Daily Mail* article on the last surviving prefab estate, Catford, South
   London.
5. 'Modernism' – Royal Institute of British Architects. https://www.architecture.com/
   Explore/ArchitecturalStyles/Modernism.aspx
   An academic article examining the Modernist architectural movement.

6. 'From Garden City to new towns: why Britons should be proud of its planners'. *Guardian*. 3 June 2014. https://www.theguardian.com/cities/2014/jun/03/from-garden-city-to-new-towns-why-britain-should-be-proud-of-its-planners
Assesses Britain's urban and suburban planning in the inter-war and post-war years.

7. Public Information Films, 1945–1951. Film Index. 'Charley in New Town' – The National Archives. 1948. http://www.nationalarchives.gov.uk/films/1945to1951/filmpage_cint.htm
An eight-minute 1948 film takes a light-hearted look at town planning in the post-war period.

8. 'The History of Council Housing'. University of West of England. UWE Bristol. https://fet.uwe.ac.uk/conweb/house_ages/council_housing/print.htm
Examines the development of council housing from the First World War into the twenty-first century.

9. Domestic Architecture 1700–1960. Post-war housing, 1945–60. Faculty of Environment and Technology. University of West of England. UWE Bristol.
Looks at housing over the centuries with a section on the 1950s boom in council housing.

10. 'Liverpool's Hardmans' House Wakes Up For A New Season'
http://www.liverpoolecho.co.uk/whats-on/arts-culture-news/liverpools-hardmans-house
Looks at a legacy of over 200,000 photographs and negatives that Liverpool photographer Chambre Hardman (1898–1988) accumulated over his lifetime – including across the 1950s. The photographs have been preserved by the National Trust in Hardman's own home, which is also open to visitors.